SHAKESPEARE'S WOR

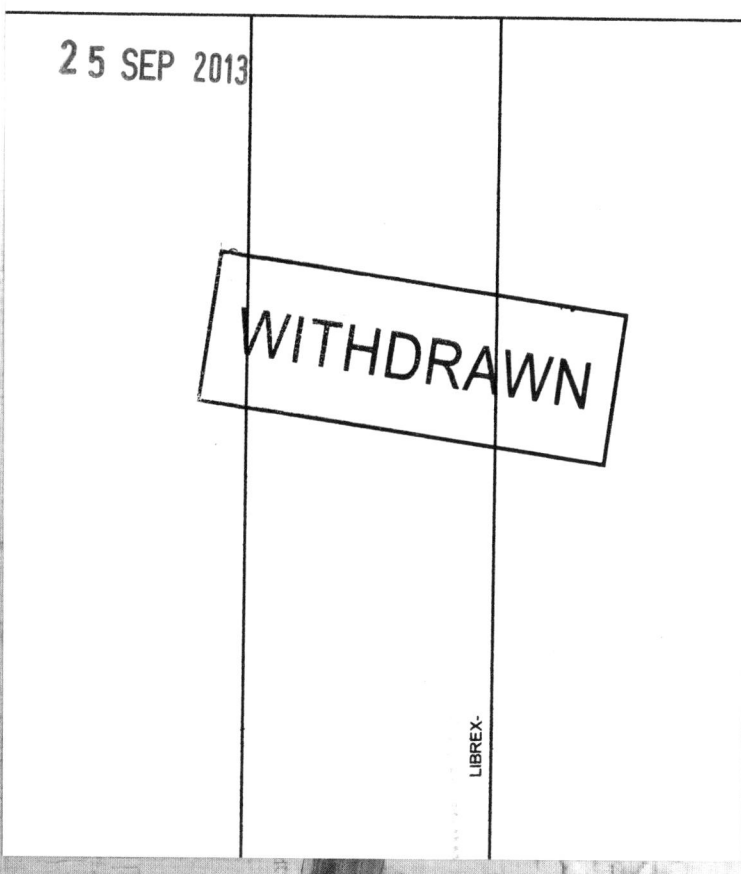
Daily Life

Kathy Elgin

CHERRYTREE BOOKS

First published in paperback in 2008

Published in Great Britain by Cherrytree Books, part of the Evans Publishing Group.

2a Portman Mansions,
Chiltern Street
London W1U 6NR

Produced for Evans Brothers by Bailey Publishing Associates Ltd
11a Woodlands
Hove BN3 6TJ

Editor: Alex Woolf
Designer: Simon Borrough
Artwork: Adam Hook
Picture research: Glass Onion Pictures

British Library Cataloguing in Publication Data
Elgin, Kathy, 1948-
Shakespeare's world : daily life
1 .Shakespeare, William, 1564-1616 - Themes, motives - Juvenile literature
2 .England - Social Conditions - 16th century - Juvenile literature 3 .England - Social life and customs - 16th century - Juvenile literature 4 .Great Britain - History - Elizabeth, 1558-1603 - Juvenile Literature
I .Title
942' 055

ISBN 9781842345177

Printed and bound in China

Titles in this series:
Daily Life
Crime and Punishment
Health and Disease
Theatre and Entertainment

Picture Acknowledgements:
The publishers would like to thank the following for permission to reproduce their pictures:
Art Archive: cover (portrait); Bridgeman Art Library: cover (background), 7 (both), 8, 11 (top), 13 (both), 14, 15, 19 (top), 22, 23, 24, 25, 27 (top), 28, 29; Mary Evans: 20, 27 (bottom); Museum of London: 17 (top); National Trust: 9, 11 (bottom), 17 (bottom); Topham/Fotomas: 19 (bottom); Victoria & Albert Museum: 21.

Contents

Introduction

Who Was Shakespeare?

William Shakespeare is probably the most famous playwright in the world. He was born in 1564 in Stratford-upon-Avon, and four hundred years after his death his plays are still being performed all over the world in almost every language you can think of. Although he came from a fairly ordinary family and didn't even go to university, he wrote thirty-eight plays with exciting plots and new, dramatic language.

Most of his plays were performed at the Globe, one of the very first theatres in London. Some were also performed for Queen Elizabeth I herself at court. Because he was also an actor and probably appeared in some of his own plays, Shakespeare knew what audiences liked. He became one of the most popular playwrights of his day and, by the time he died in 1616, he was a wealthy man.

Daily Life in Shakespeare's Time

The sixteenth century was a time of enormous change in England. Queen Elizabeth's long reign brought peace and prosperity, and England was becoming a great world power. London was a bustling centre for all kinds of trade, with fortunes to be made for enterprising people. Now it wasn't only the old aristocratic families who had money — the rising "middle classes" were getting rich as well through business.

Although most people still lived in the countryside, England was becoming more industrial and the people who moved into towns to look for work were often very poor. Living first in a small market town and then in London, Shakespeare experienced all this himself.

Although a lot of Shakespeare's plays are set in foreign countries and historical times — Scotland for *Macbeth*, Denmark for *Hamlet*, ancient Rome for *Julius Caesar*, and so on — when he wrote them he was actually taking his inspiration from the people he saw around him and what was happening in his own times.

Of course, there were no recent history books to tell him how people really behaved in ancient Rome, or how they spoke, so he had to look around him and base his characters on the people he met every day in London or Stratford. It's as if he was writing about Elizabethan England "in disguise", and because of this, a lot of the words and images Shakespeare uses can tell us a good deal about sixteenth-century England.

Love and Marriage

In Shakespeare's day, falling in love and getting married were two very different matters, especially for the upper classes. Marriage had more to do with money than with love, and most marriages were arranged in order to bring wealth into a family. Because of this, young people often had to marry the person chosen by their parents. Poorer people were generally free to make their own choices. Many could not afford a church wedding but simply made promises to each other in the presence of witnesses, which was considered a legal marriage.

Even if she had chosen someone quite suitable as a husband, a girl could not marry without her father's consent.

I come to wive it wealthily in Padua;
If wealthily, then happily in Padua.
THE TAMING OF THE SHREW,
ACT 1, SCENE 2

wive it: marry a wife

Petruchio, quoted here, has only one thing on his mind where marriage is concerned — he wants a wife with a good fortune. Marriage was the best way for Elizabethan men to restore their family wealth. Some girls from rich families were treated more like valuable objects than like daughters, and were often "sold off" to the highest bidder, sometimes to men they had never met. Not surprisingly, many of these marriages proved unhappy, but divorce was almost impossible.

Lies my consent and fair according voice.

> *But woo her, gentle Paris, get her heart,*
> *My will to her consent is but a part;*
> *An she agree, within her scope of choice*
> *Lies my consent and fair according voice.*
>
> ROMEO AND JULIET, ACT 1, SCENE 2

woo: court
an: if

Couples were often engaged for a long time before marrying, so they gave each other brooches or rings containing a lock of hair as keepsakes.

In this passage, Juliet's father has already decided that the wealthy young Paris is suitable, but he makes it clear that the wedding will only go ahead if Juliet agrees. Most parents wanted their children to be happy and preferred them to marry someone they loved, as Juliet's father does. Engagements were often arranged when girls were very young, even if they didn't actually go to live with their husbands until later. Juliet is not quite fourteen when her parents start to plan her marriage.

Upper-class weddings were celebrated in splendid fashion with music, dancing and elaborate theatrical performances.

The Family

Family life was more strict than it is today. The father was the head of the household and demanded obedience from his wife and children. In wealthy families, parents often did not see much of their children until they were older, as they were looked after by servants. In some wealthy families, wives actually took control of the household when their husbands were called away to the army or travelled on business.

Some of the time parents spent with their children was used for Bible reading and family prayers, as well as games that trained them for later life.

Thy husband is thy lord, thy life, thy keeper,
Thy head, thy sovereign…
THE TAMING OF THE SHREW, ACT 5, SCENE 2

sovereign: king

Katherina, in this quote from the end of *The Taming of the Shrew*, is reminding other women of their duty to their husbands. Scripture taught that the family was a model of the church, or the kingdom. The father was the highest authority and his wife and children were all meant to respect him in the same way that people respected and looked up to God and to the king.

Here are some of the thirteen children of Sir Thomas Lucy. Because boys and girls were dressed alike until the age of about seven, it is difficult to tell which is which.

Although the father was head of the family, it was often the wife's duty to discipline the children.

Your children were vexation to your youth,
But mine shall be a comfort to your age.
Richard III, Act 4, Scene 4

vexation: a nuisance
age: old age

Because there were no pensions or social services in Shakespeare's day, children were supposed to look after their parents in their old age. Parents tended to have a lot of children because so many did not survive childhood, especially in poor families. Shakespeare's own son Hamnet died at the age of eleven, and Juliet's father tells us that she is his only surviving child. On average, people did not live as long as we do today and they were thought of as "old" if they reached their fifties.

But mine shall be a comfort to your age.

Houses and Gardens

In big, overcrowded cities like London, most of the housing for ordinary people was poor, with tall, rough houses built close together. They were dark and had few windows. Wealthy people, however, had fine houses filled with beautiful furniture. Many of the newly rich people built elegant manor houses in the country. These houses had all the latest features, like glass windows and chimneys.

Elizabethans also grew plants for use in cooking and, especially, in medicines. Most houses had a herb garden as well as flowers.

My house within the city
Is richly furnished....
My hangings all of Tyrian tapestry.
In ivory coffers I have stuff'd my crowns,
In cypress chests my arras counterpoints,
Costly apparel, tents and canopies,
Fine linen, Turkey cushions boss'd with pearl....
THE TAMING OF THE SHREW, ACT 2, SCENE 1

hangings: tapestry panels to hang on the wall
Tyrian: from Tyre, famous for its scarlet dye
coffer: chest
arras counterpoint: bedspread woven at Arras in France
boss'd: embossed, embroidered
crowns: coins

In this passage, Gremio, a rich old man, talks proudly of all the luxury items like tapestries, cushions and embroidered fabrics that he has had imported from the Far East or Italy to make his home comfortable. Well-off Elizabethans liked to show off their wealth by having fine furniture and the latest fashionable objects on display in their homes.

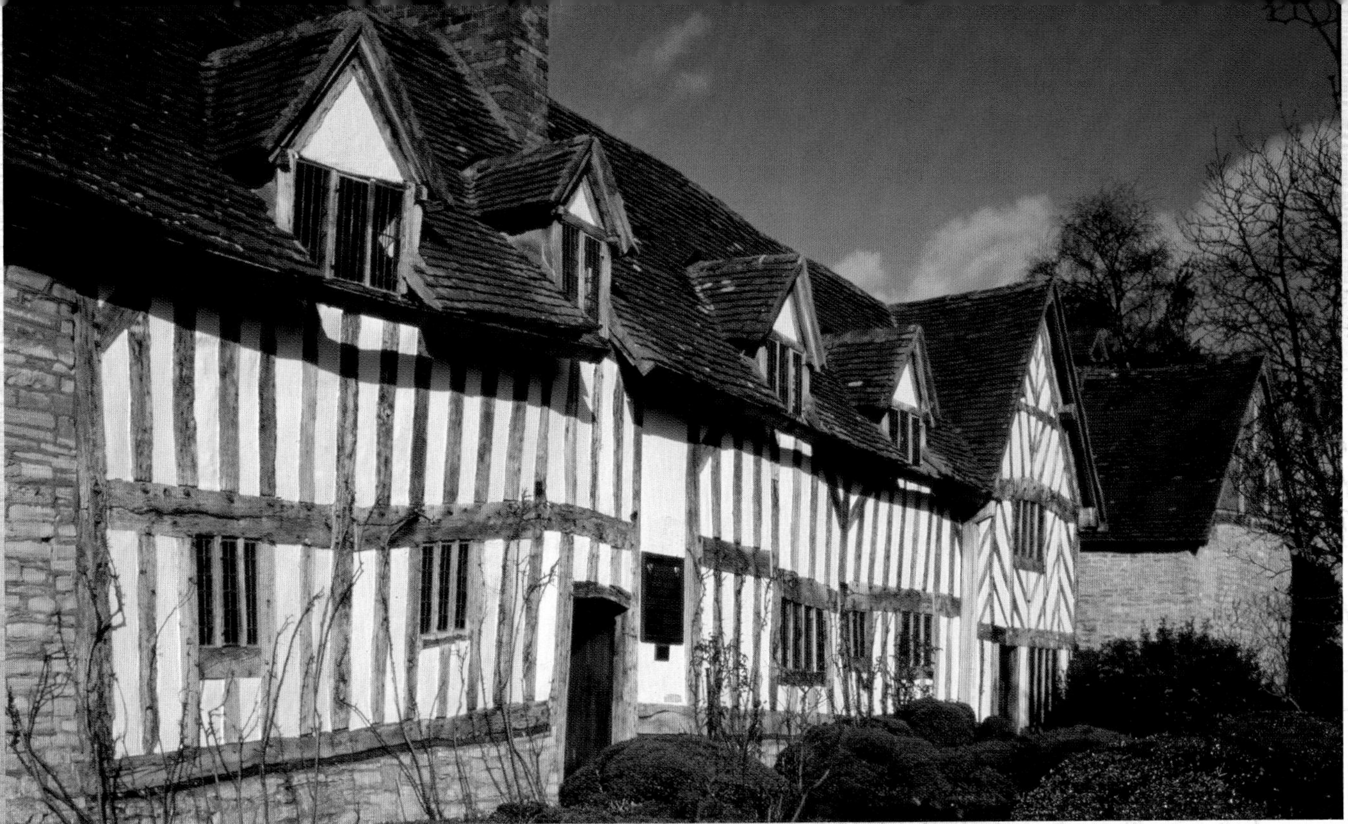

A typical Elizabethan house like this one (which may have been the home of Mary Arden, Shakespeare's mother) was built of timber frame and plaster.

> *In emerald tufts, flowers purple, blue and white;*
> *Like sapphire, pearl, and rich embroidery....*
> *Fairies use flowers for their charactery.*
>
> THE MERRY WIVES OF WINDSOR, ACT 5, SCENE 5

charactery: script

The fairies in this play are planting a garden to look like living embroidery. Gardens were an obvious way of displaying wealth because they could be seen by everyone who passed by, not just the friends who were invited inside the house. Elizabethans were enthusiastic gardeners, cultivating formal gardens with tree-lined walks. Knot gardens were especially popular. These contained elaborate patterns formed by planting an outline of small hedges and filling in the gaps with brightly coloured flowers.

In knot gardens, like this one at Mosely Old Hall, the hedges were of fragrant rosemary, lavender or dwarf box, filled in with flowers or coloured gravel.

Servants and Housework

The great houses needed armies of servants to keep them going, but even relatively modest households kept servants. There would be maids to do the cleaning, a cook and perhaps scullery maids in the kitchen, and odd-job servants to do the shopping and run errands. Better-off families would also have a nurse to feed and look after the babies and small children.

Wealthy people often employed their poorer relations as servants, enabling them to improve their position in society.

I may call him my master, look you, for I keep his house; and I wash, wring, brew, bake, scour, dress meat and drink, make the beds and do all myself....

THE MERRY WIVES OF WINDSOR, ACT 1, SCENE 4

scour: clean or polish
dress: get food ready for the table
meat: food in general

The characters in this play are middle-class families of Shakespeare's own time. They all keep servants, including Mistress Quickly, who tells us about her average day's housework. This includes doing the laundry, cleaning the house, brewing ale and baking bread every day. Her master, the doctor, is obviously not well-off, as Mistress Quickly has to do all this work herself.

make the beds and do all myself....

The kitchen of a big house was hot, noisy, full of activity, and often hazardous, as much of the cooking was done on open fires.

Look here is a basket ... he may creep in here; and throw foul linen upon him, as it were going to bucking: or — it is whiting time — send him by your two men to Datchet-mead.

THE MERRY WIVES OF WINDSOR, ACT 3, SCENE 3

foul: dirty
bucking: soaking clothes for the wash
whiting time: time for bleaching clothes
mead: meadow

Mrs Ford is helping Falstaff to escape by hiding him in the linen basket. Dirty washing could be sent to the launderers, where clothes were washed by hand, with a lot of soaking and scrubbing. In country areas clothes and household linen could be hung over hedges to dry and bleach in the sun. This was a risky business, however, because frequently the clothes were stolen by passing thieves, who then sold them.

Most towns and villages had a public washing ground where, on one day a week, the women would chat and exchange news as they did their laundry.

Food and Drink

Elizabethan meals seem enormous to us. There could easily be over a dozen courses, especially if the family had guests. Roast meat was followed by several different sorts of poultry, then pies, salads and vegetables, and after all that, sweet tarts, creamy syllabubs, fruit and nuts. Working people had less variety and the poor sometimes had little more than bread and cheese. Country people grew most of their own food and kept their own animals for eating.

Let me see; what am I to buy for our sheep-shearing feast? Three pound of sugar; five pound of currants; rice.... I must have saffron, to colour the warden pies; mace, dates ... nutmegs seven; a race or two of ginger — but that I may beg — four pound of prunes, and as many of raisins o' the sun.

THE WINTER'S TALE, ACT 4, SCENE 3

warden pies: sweet pies made of warden pears
mace: spice made from nutmeg
race: root
raisins o' the sun: grapes dried in the sun

This is a typical shopping list. Herbs and spices were used to give flavour and sometimes to hide the taste of stale food, and sugar was used to sweeten wine. The Elizabethans liked rich, spicy puddings — rather like Christmas puddings of today — which would keep for a long time.

Even families who could afford meat depended on bread as a main part of their meal and used it to wipe up sauces.

Most ordinary people ate off wooden plates or "trenchers" and used simple pottery jugs like these for their ale.

It was usual for people to bring their own knives and spoons to the table, and eating with the fingers was not considered rude.

You rogue, there's lime in this sack!
HENRY IV PART 1,
ACT 2, SCENE 4

sack: sherry

Tea and coffee were not yet known in England and clean drinking water was rare, so men and women alike generally drank ale or beer at mealtimes. This was only mildly alcoholic, and most households brewed their own. Another drink was sack, a kind of sherry, which was sold in taverns. Customers, like Falstaff in this play, were always complaining that the landlord had watered down their drink or put lime in it, to make it more dry and sparkling.

Clothes and Fashion

Elizabethan clothes, for most people except the very poor, were highly elaborate. Women's dresses, made of silk or velvet and covered with rich embroidery, went down to their ankles and had a frame underneath to make the skirts stand out. Men wore a short embroidered doublet, tights and fancy shoes with high heels. Collars and ruffs, made of lace and stiffened with starch, were very popular. Elaborate hairstyles and powdered wigs dressed with ribbons and jewels made up for the fact that people hardly ever washed their hair.

> *Costly thy habit as thy purse can buy,*
> *But not express'd in fancy; rich, not gaudy:*
> *For the apparel oft proclaims the man.*
> HAMLET, ACT 1, SCENE 3

habit: clothing
fancy: ornamentation
apparel: clothing

Here Polonius is warning his son about showing off by wearing over-elaborate clothes which will make him look silly. Men in Shakespeare's day thought as much about clothes as women, particularly at the royal court, and playwrights often made fun of them. Eventually, men's hats became so ridiculous that laws were passed limiting their decoration.

Better-off Elizabethans, being very fashion conscious, were always looking out for new styles and fabrics from Italy, France or Spain.

To appear in public, men liked to be properly dressed in full formal attire, with hat, cloak and gloves. Some paintings show that they kept these on indoors.

> … a certain lord, neat, and trimly dress'd,
> Fresh as a bridegroom; and his chin, new reap'd,
> Show'd like a stubble-land at harvest-home:
> He was perfumed like a milliner,
> And 'twixt his finger and his thumb he held
> A pouncet-box, which ever and anon
> He gave his nose and took't away again;
>
> HENRY IV PART 1, ACT 1, SCENE 3

reap'd: shaved
milliner: someone who makes hats for women
'twixt: between
pouncet-box: box with herbal powder, possibly to ward off the plague

Once boys and girls stopped wearing their identical baby clothes, they were dressed like small adults in miniature versions of their parents' elaborate outfits.

This man is a typical courtier. He is clean-shaven, although beards were also fashionable, and like most men and women, he is wearing perfume. Although their clothes were fine, even rich people hardly ever took baths, and the perfume must have covered up some powerful smells. They also carried little boxes of aromatic powder. They believed that sniffing this would protect them from the plague.

Schools and Education

Elizabethan children went first to the "petty school" (from the French word *petit*, meaning "little") to learn spelling, reading and counting. When they were eleven they went to a grammar school where they learned Latin, English grammar, Bible study and some history. Instead of being taught about their own times they studied the lives of great men as examples of good behaviour which they should imitate. They also practised debating and making speeches. The better-off boys, who intended to be lawyers or priests, could go on to university at Oxford or Cambridge. Girls did not have these opportunities.

The Elizabethans were passionate about education and encouraged the founding of grammar schools in many towns for the children of less well-off families.

Schoolmasters will I keep within my house,
Fit to instruct her youth.
THE TAMING OF THE SHREW, ACT 1, SCENE 1

Wealthy households employed private tutors, who taught extra subjects like music, dancing and drawing. However, many poor children got no education at all and were not able to read. For girls — even those from wealthier families — education was generally considered a waste of time and they were taught practical subjects like sewing and cooking, which would be useful in running a home after they were married.

Creeping like snail Unwillingly to school.

Then, the whining school-boy, with his satchel,
And shining morning face, creeping like snail
Unwillingly to school.

AS YOU LIKE IT, ACT 2, SCENE 7

A lot of schoolwork involved copying out exercises, learning things by heart and repeating in chorus what the master told them.

This little girl is learning from a hornbook, a framed piece of thin animal horn on which an alphabet or a religious text was written.

Obviously school was no more popular in Shakespeare's day than it is now! Perhaps it's not surprising. In his time it was hard work, and because of all the learning by heart, not very exciting. The school day was long, from six o'clock in the morning to five in the evening, six days a week, and apart from Christmas and Easter there were not many holidays. There are several schoolmasters in Shakespeare's plays, possibly based on his own teacher, Mr Jenkins, at Stratford grammar school.

Sports and Hobbies

Elizabethan men enjoyed all kinds of competitive physical sports like riding, wrestling and fencing, where they could show off their strength and skill. Country sports like hunting, fishing and hawking were popular with both rich and poor. Many women, including Queen Elizabeth, also took part in sports like riding and archery, but in general they were expected to have more modest, indoor pastimes such as reading, playing musical instruments and sewing.

> *Am I so round with you, as you with me,*
> *That like a football you do spurn me thus?*
> *You spurn me hence, and he will spurn me hither:*
> *If I last in this service you must case me in leather.*
> THE COMEDY OF ERRORS, ACT 2, SCENE 1

round: harsh
spurn: kick

Football was already a popular game, especially in the country, where village teams challenged each other. However, because there could be any number of people on each team, it was a chaotic and dangerous game and people were often seriously injured. King James himself warned his son against taking part in such a rough sport. Characters in Shakespeare's plays also take part in sports such as tennis, bowling and greyhound racing.

Country football was dangerous but it was even worse for townspeople who had to get out of the way of young men rushing through the narrow streets.

sampler: needlework panel with patterns, alphabet letters and many different stitches

> We, Hermia, like two artificial gods,
> Have with our needles created both one flower,
> Both on one sampler, sitting on one cushion....
> A MIDSUMMER NIGHT'S DREAM, ACT 3, SCENE 2

Different breeds of hawk were thought to be suitable for different social classes – a peregrine for an earl, a goshawk for a wealthy farmer, a kestrel for a poor man.

Needlework was an ideal pastime for girls because it was quiet and kept them out of mischief, but also produced useful things. They embroidered sheets and household linen for their wedding trousseau (a bride's clothes and linen), and even when they were married they always needed new cushions, wall hangings and curtains to keep the place warm. Even girls as young as six or seven embroidered samplers, to teach them how to do different stitches.

Samplers, often worked by girls as young as eight or nine, showed letters of the alphabet, images of flowers and fruit or sometimes just patterns of different stitches.

Entertainment

In Shakespeare's day, the theatre was fast becoming a favourite with all classes of society. Troupes of players travelled the country and set up their stages in inn-yards, while in London large permanent theatres were being built, where people could see a different play every night. Writers like Shakespeare were always busy keeping up with demand for new plays. Next door to the theatre — or sometimes even in the same building — were cruel and dangerous sports involving wild animals. Elizabethans seem to have enjoyed these just as much as plays.

If music be the food of love, play on,
Give me excess of it, that, surfeiting,
The appetite may sicken, and so die.
TWELFTH NIGHT, ACT 1, SCENE 1

surfeiting: having too much

Music and dancing were an important part of life. People enjoyed music at church, and at home almost everybody could play an instrument. Refined people played the virginal, a kind of harpsichord, or the lute, while at village celebrations you were more likely to hear drums, horns and bagpipes. At weddings and other celebrations there was always dancing, which often became lively as people tried out the latest dance steps from Italy and France.

The Elizabethans loved music and dancing. At court they welcomed any opportunity to dress up and take part in amateur theatricals.

I have seen Sackerson [a bear] loose twenty times, and have taken him by the chain; but, I warrant you, the women have so cried and shrieked at it that it passed: but women indeed cannot abide 'em; they are very ill-favoured rough things.

THE MERRY WIVES OF WINDSOR, ACT I, SCENE 1

warrant: promise
passed: surpassed, was very remarkable

Some of the actors in Shakespeare's company, like the clown Will Kempe, were as famous as television stars today.

People flocked to bear-baiting and bull-baiting, when wild animals were set loose in a pit to be attacked by savage dogs. Young men liked to test their courage by getting up close to an angry bear. Sackerson was a particularly famous bear, kept in London, which had killed several men. Cock-fighting and dog-fighting were other violent sports that were popular at the time.

Bear and bull-baiting, which usually took place on a Sunday, was a respectable sport enjoyed by all classes and even Queen Elizabeth herself.

Town and Country

In Shakespeare's day there was a big division between town and country people. Because they didn't mix much, each had little idea how the others lived and they tended to be rather suspicious of each other. Townspeople thought of country folk as honest but sometimes simpleminded, perhaps because few of them had much education. Towns were thought to be violent, noisy places, teeming with pickpockets and other criminals.

There were harsh penalties for all kinds of criminals, including this beggar, who is being whipped through the streets.

old custom: a long time
painted pomp: artificial splendour
envious: where envy is common

> *Hath not old custom made this life more sweet*
> *Than that of painted pomp? Are not these woods*
> *More free from peril than the envious court?*
> As You Like It, Act 2, Scene 1

In the late sixteenth century, woodland and forest still covered a lot of the land. Shakespeare uses forests not just as beautiful, unspoiled retreats, but as magical places where mysterious things can happen, as they do in *As You Like It*. Here the Duke has been banished from court and gone to live in the Forest of Arden, where he is trying to persuade his men that this simple country life is preferable to their old life amongst the deceitful courtiers.

> *When icicles hang by the wall,*
> *And Dick the shepherd blows his nail,*
> *And Tom bears logs into the hall,*
> *And milk comes frozen home in pail....*
>   LOVE'S LABOUR'S LOST, ACT 5,
>   SCENE 2

Whatever townspeople thought, in reality country life was hard, and people were at the mercy of the weather and the seasons. The working day began early, as soon as the sun came up, and did not end until it got dark. In winter, with only log fires for heating, life could be very difficult in both town and country.

Most people in Shakespeare's England still worked on the land, although sheep farming was beginning to take over from growing corn and wheat.

The Elizabethans liked to think of the countryside as a place of innocence and simple pleasures: the plays and poems of the time are full of contented shepherds.

Travel

Travelling was a hazardous business. The roads were bad and travellers were always at risk from robbers. Most people who lived and worked within their own small area got about on foot. If they had to go further afield, they paid to travel with their luggage in the carrier's cart, which went back and forth between towns. The better-off travelled on horseback or in their own horse-drawn coaches.

There are pilgrims going to Canterbury with rich offerings, and traders riding to London with fat purses: I have vizards for you all; you have horses for yourselves....
HENRY IV PART I, ACT 1, SCENE 2

vizards: masks

Bedrooms might be uncomfortable but travellers could usually depend on a welcome pint of ale and hot food at the inn.

A lot of people went on religious pilgrimages to various shrines around the country, such as Walsingham in Norfolk or the shrine of St Thomas at Canterbury in Kent, hoping to be cured of ailments. These travellers, usually on foot, were easy prey for the masked highwaymen lying in wait by the roadside, as in this play. Other frequent travellers were farmers who had to get their goods to market, and rich merchants heading for London to buy and sell.

Country roads were often no better than tracks worn by frequent passage of the carrier's cart, and bad weather made them impassable.

The west yet glimmers with some streaks of day;
Now spurs the lated traveller apace
To gain the timely inn.

MACBETH, ACT 3, SCENE 3

lated: belated
apace: quickly
gain: reach
timely: in good time

Travelling was particularly dangerous after dark, and sensible people made sure they reached home or an inn before sundown. However, inns were usually not very comfortable. You shared a room — and quite often a bed! — with any strangers who happened to arrive at the same time. The bedding was frequently dirty and you were likely to wake up in the morning bitten by fleas. Most people were glad to eat their breakfast of bread, cheese and ale and get on with their journey.

The open heath, where this highwayman is robbing a peddler, was an especially dangerous place for travellers.

Old Age

It was quite an achievement for an Elizabethan to reach old age, especially for poorer people. Accidents and illness — especially frequent outbreaks of the plague — carried off people from all classes long before they reached their forties. Even if they survived, old age was not always enjoyable. Women who survived childbirth generally lived longer than men and so they were frequently left as widows. Sometimes, because they were now independent and had no husband to control them, they were considered a bad influence in society.

A MOST Certain, Strange, and true Discovery of a VVITCH.

Being taken by some of the Parliament Forces, as she was standing on a small planck board and sayling on it over the River of *Newbury*:

Together with the strange and true manner of her death, with the propheticall words and speeches she used at the same time.

Printed by John Hammond, 1643.

> *... that which should accompany old age,*
> *As honour, love, obedience, troops of friends,*
> *I must not look to have.*
>
> MACBETH, ACT 5, SCENE 3

look: expect

Elderly women living alone were often accused of being witches and were persecuted by their neighbours. Sometimes they were even tried and put to death.

Traditionally, old men were looked up to by their families and enjoyed a special place in society. Because they had managed to survive into old age, their long experience gave them dignity and entitled them to respect. Here Macbeth, who has committed some terrible murders, knows that he is about to be killed and realizes that he will never reach that happy stage of life that most men looked forward to.

apply Hot and rebellious liquors....

Though I look old, I am strong and lusty;
For in my youth I never did apply
Hot and rebellious liquors....
Therefore my age is as a lusty winter,
Frosty but kindly.

AS YOU LIKE IT, ACT 2, SCENE 3

lusty: strong
rebellious: upsetting
the healthy working
of the body

Old Adam is keen to persuade his young master that he is still fit and healthy, and says this is because he did not get drunk in his younger days. Old servants who could no longer work were often turned out of the house to fend for themselves and many ended their lives as beggars. In this play, though, Adam has a kind master who takes care of him.

In As You Like It *Shakespeare imagines the life of man at seven different ages, ranging from a baby to an old man. This painting shows the same idea.*

If they were lucky, old people might live out their days in an almshouse, a kind of hostel supported by wealthy patrons.

Timeline

1533 — Princess Elizabeth, daughter of King Henry VIII, is born.

1551 — First licensing of ale houses in England.

1554 — Under the new queen, Mary, Roman Catholicism is re-established in England.

1558 — Elizabeth becomes queen.

1563 — Plague, spreading from Europe, kills 20,000 people in London.

1564 — Shakespeare is born.

1565 — Tobacco is first introduced to England.

1566 — London's Royal Exchange, a shopping and trading centre, is founded by Thomas Gresham.

1570 — The potato is introduced to Europe from Spanish America.

1572 — A law is passed for the punishment of vagrants.

1576 — Another Act of Parliament establishes houses of correction and hard labour for vagrants and thieves.
The Theatre — London's first permanent theatre — opens on the banks of the Thames.

1577 — Sir Francis Drake sets off on his voyage round the world.

1580 — New building in London is forbidden in an attempt to restrict the growth of the city.

1585 — Sir Walter Raleigh's first colony is established in Roanoke, Virginia, in newly discovered America.

1587 — Mary Queen of Scots is executed after being implicated in a plot to kill Queen Elizabeth.

1588 — Defeat of the Spanish Armada: England is saved from invasion.

1594 — Poor grain harvests increase the price of bread, the main food of the poor.

1597 — King James of Scotland publishes a book on witchcraft.

1598 — New Poor Laws are passed to take care of the poor.

1599 — The Globe, Shakespeare's theatre, opens.

1600 — The East India Company is established, opening up trade with India and the east.
The population of England and Ireland is now five and a half million.

1601 — Poor Law statutes compel each parish to provide work for the unemployed.

1603 — The death of Queen Elizabeth and accession of James I.

1604 — Peace treaty with Spain.

1605 — 5 November: the Gunpowder Plot to blow up Parliament is discovered.

1607 — Foundation of the English colony of Jamestown, Virginia, under Captain John Smith.

1609 — Tea is first shipped to Europe from China.

1612 — Witchcraft trials in Pendle, Lancashire, condemn many women to burning.

1613 — The cutting of the New River brings a cleaner water supply to London.
The Globe is destroyed by fire.

1615 — *The English Housewife*, a cookery book and general household manual, is published.

1616 — Shakespeare dies.

1618 — King James' *Book of Sports* encourages the playing of various sports, to the fury of the Puritans.

1620 — The Pilgrim Fathers sail for America in the *Mayflower* to found Plymouth colony.

Glossary

Further Information

Difficult Shakespearean words appear alongside each quotation. This glossary explains words used in the main text.

bawdy	Vulgar or rude.
courtier	An officer or attendant at court.
doublet	A short jacket for men.
embroidery	Decorative needlework on cloth.
fencing	The sport of fighting with swords.
grammar school	A secondary school teaching academic subjects.
harpsichord	An early form of piano but with plucked strings.
hawking	Hunting with birds of prey.
inn-yard	The courtyard of an inn where coaches pulled in.
lute	A pear-shaped stringed instrument to be strummed.
madrigal	A song in which several people sing different parts, usually unaccompanied.
merchant	A tradesman or salesman.
middle classes	The reasonably well-off people who were not members of the aristocracy. The middle classes included businesspeople, professionals and skilled workers.
pension	A payment from the state to the old or those unable to work.
plague	A highly infectious disease, spread by rats, that made frequent appearances during the medieval and Tudor periods, killing large numbers of people.
ruff	An elaborately pleated, circular collar.
scullery maid	A kitchen maid who did the cleaning and washing up.
starch	A liquid used to stiffen fabric.
syllabub	A dessert made of cream beaten with sugar, wine and lemon juice.
tapestry	A woven or embroidered picture.
tavern	An inn or public house.
trousseau	Clothes and household linen collected by a bride for her wedding.
upper classes	The better-off members of society; also known as the aristocracy.
virginal	A kind of harpsichord.

Further Reading

The Best Loved Plays of Shakespeare by Abigail Frost and Jennifer Mulherin (Cherrytree Books, 1997)
Sightseers Shakespeare (Kingfisher Books, 2002)
Shakespeare's Storybook by Patrick Ryan (Barefoot Books, 2001)
Eyewitness: Shakespeare by Peter Chrisp (Dorling Kindersley, 2002)
Look Inside a Shakespearean Theatre by Peter Chrisp (Hodder Wayland, 2000)
The Illustrated World of the Tudors by Peter Chrisp (Hodder Wayland, 2001)
Shakespeare and the Elizabethan Age by Andrew Langley (Treasure Chest, 2000)
The Usborne World of Shakespeare by Anna Claybourne (Usborne, 2001)

Video, DVD and CD-Rom

All Shakespeare's plays are available in several versions from the Royal Shakespeare Company and can be ordered from their website (see below)
Complete Works of Shakespeare on CD-Rom (Focus Multimedia)

Websites

www.rsc.org.uk
Royal Shakespeare Company. Contains information about plays and education projects.

www.shakespeare.org.uk
Shakespeare Birthplace Trust.
Contains background
information on Shakespeare,
his life and times.

Index